WHAT'S INSIDE?

INSECTS

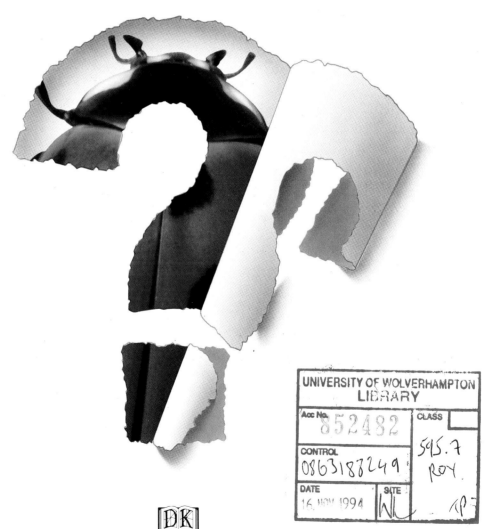

DK

DORLING KINDERSLEY
LONDON • NEW YORK • STUTTGART

BEETLE

This is a snout beetle. It is called this because of its big, funny 'nose'. Its jaws are at the end and it uses them to eat plants.

Like all insects, the beetle has six legs. They have joints like our knees or elbows.

Here are the beetle's eyes.

Here are the beetle's antennae.

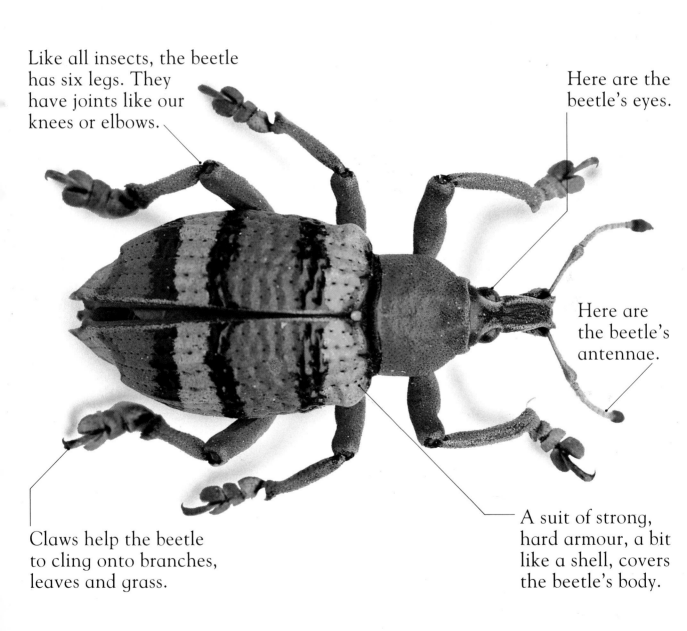

Claws help the beetle to cling onto branches, leaves and grass.

A suit of strong, hard armour, a bit like a shell, covers the beetle's body.

3/94

IIVE

A Dorling Kindersley Book
Conceived, edited and designed by DK Direct Limited

Note to parents

What's Inside? Insects is designed to help young children understand the fascinating secrets of insects' bodies. It shows what is inside a caterpillar, how a spiny stick insect lays eggs and how a fly can walk on the ceiling. It is a book for you and your child to read and talk about together, and to enjoy.

Designers   Sonia Whillock and Juliette Norsworthy
Typographic Designer   Nigel Coath
Editor   Sarah Phillips
Design Director   Ed Day
Editorial Director   Jonathan Reed

Illustrator   Richard Manning
Photographer   Frank Greenaway
Writer   Angela Royston

Insects supplied by the Natural History Museum, London and Trevor Smith's Animal World

First published in Great Britain in 1992
by Dorling Kindersley Limited,
9 Henrietta Street, London WC2E 8PS

A CIP catalogue record for this book is available from the British Library.

ISBN 0-86318-824-9

Printed in Italy

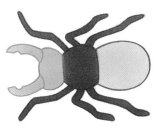

A beetle is an insect. Like all insects, it has three parts to its body: a head, a middle part, called the thorax, and a back part, called the abdomen.

Inside the beetle's hard shell, its body is soft. All parts of the body need blood, to bring food and take away waste.

This is the beetle's brain.

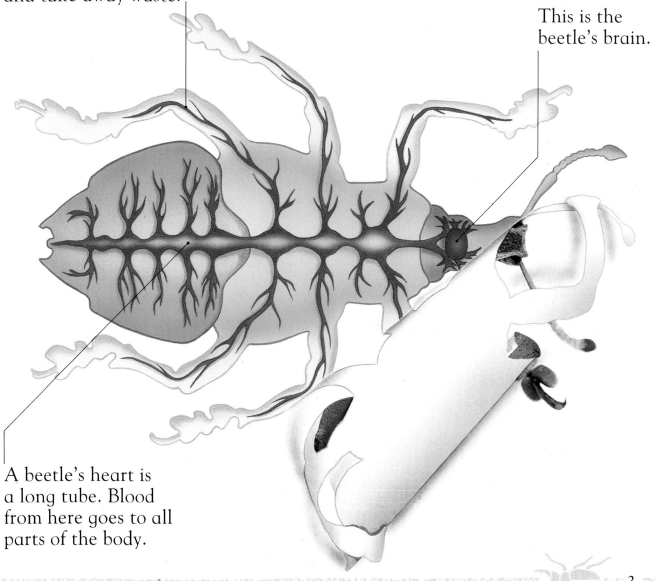

A beetle's heart is a long tube. Blood from here goes to all parts of the body.

HONEYBEE

This honeybee lives in a hive with many other bees. She feeds on pollen and nectar which she collects from flowers. Both pollen and nectar are stored inside the hive, where the nectar is made into honey.

Black and yellow stripes warn birds and other animals that bees have a poisonous sting.

The bee sucks up sweet nectar with her long tongue.

The honeybee's body is covered with hair. Pollen sticks to the hairs as the bee pushes into the centre of the flower.

Inside the hive are lots of rooms, where the honey and pollen are stored.

Poison for the bee's sting is made here. It is the poison that makes the sting hurt.

This is the bee's honey stomach. She stores the nectar here until she takes it back to the hive.

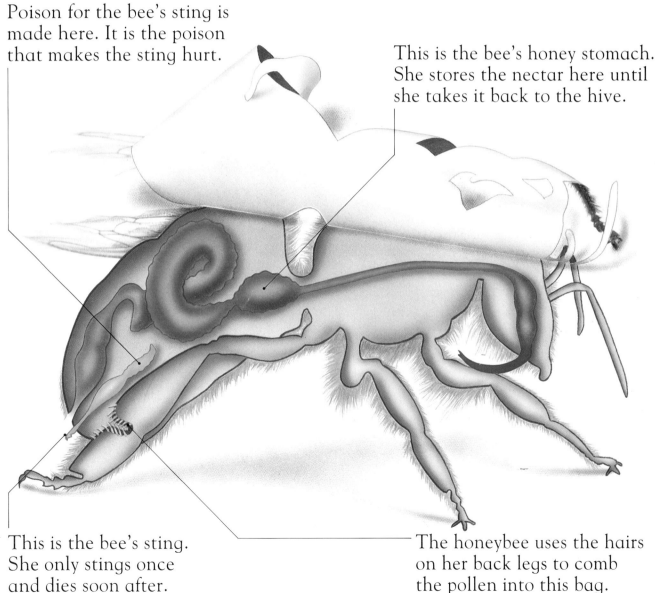

This is the bee's sting. She only stings once and dies soon after.

The honeybee uses the hairs on her back legs to comb the pollen into this bag.

CATERPILLAR

Like all insects, this caterpillar hatched out of an egg. Now it lives on leaves and spends most of its time eating. It is growing fast. Soon it will begin to change into a butterfly.

The caterpillar breathes through these holes along its side.

As it grows, a caterpillar gets too big for its skin. First a new, larger skin grows underneath, then the old skin splits and the caterpillar crawls out and leaves it behind.

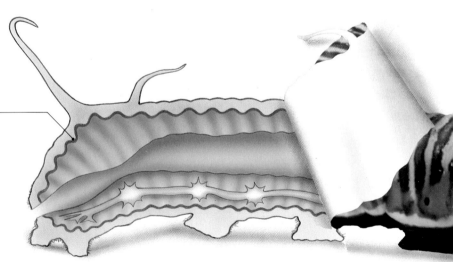

Birds leave this caterpillar alone. Its bright colours and tentacles trick them into thinking it's poisonous.

The caterpillar holds food with its front three pairs of legs. The other legs are for walking and holding on to leaves.

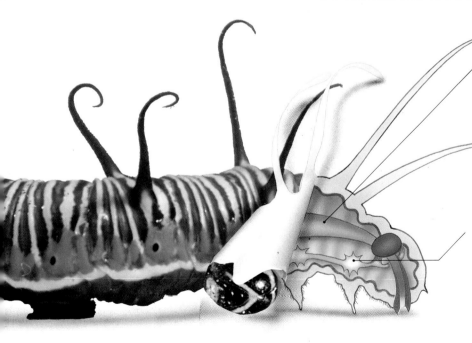

This is the caterpillar's food tube. It is very big because the caterpillar eats so much.

Nerves from here spread all over its body, so that the caterpillar can feel things around it.

FLY

Have you ever wanted to walk on the ceiling like a fly? You would have to have a fly's sticky feet to do so. Many people kill flies because they spread germs.

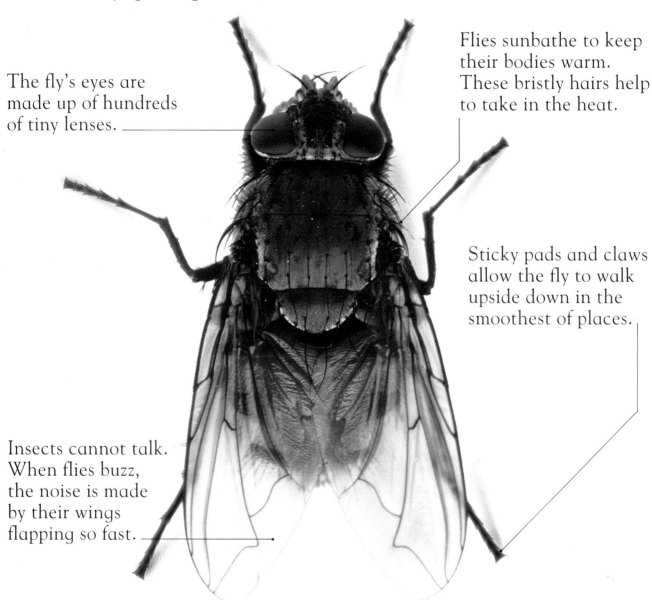

The fly's eyes are made up of hundreds of tiny lenses.

Flies sunbathe to keep their bodies warm. These bristly hairs help to take in the heat.

Sticky pads and claws allow the fly to walk upside down in the smoothest of places.

Insects cannot talk. When flies buzz, the noise is made by their wings flapping so fast.

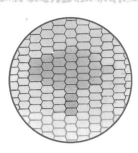

When a fly looks at something, it sees it broken up into lots and lots of little pieces, like a mosaic.

The fly breathes in and out through holes in its sides, called spiracles.

These are the fly's air sacs. They carry air to all parts of the body.

This fly, like some other insects, can taste with its feet.

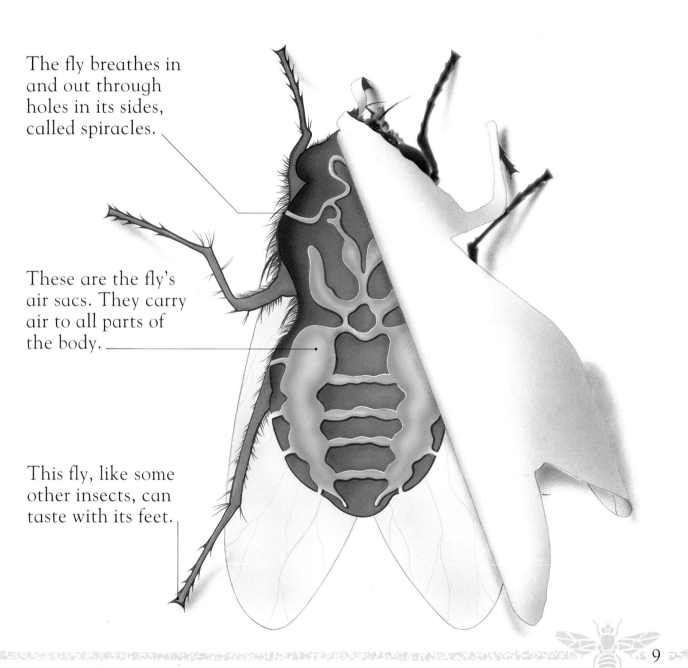

CRICKET

This bush cricket lives in rough, grassy places.
She comes out in the evening and eats plants.
If there is any danger, she'll quickly hop away.

This cricket is green, just like the grass, which helps her to hide from birds that would like to eat her.

Long antennae tell the cricket what the things around her feel and smell like.

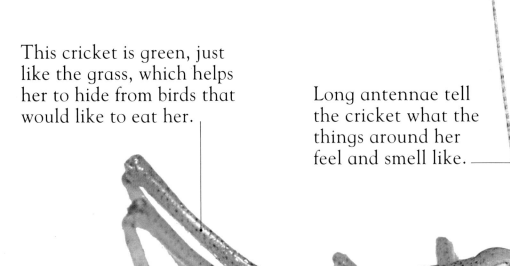

Crickets use their long back legs to leap away from danger.

Crickets have 'ears' on their front legs.

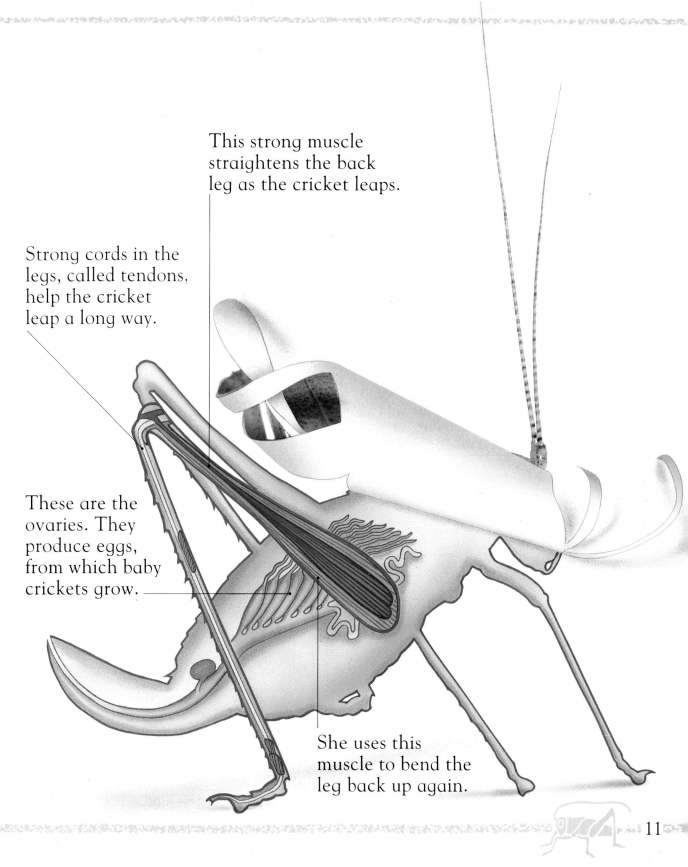

This strong muscle straightens the back leg as the cricket leaps.

Strong cords in the legs, called tendons, help the cricket leap a long way.

These are the ovaries. They produce eggs, from which baby crickets grow.

She uses this muscle to bend the leg back up again.

11

LADYBIRD

Ladybirds are a kind of beetle. They live in forests, fields, parks and gardens. Gardeners like ladybirds because they eat the greenflies that feed on garden plants.

Ladybirds are brightly coloured to warn birds and other animals that they taste nasty.

Not all ladybirds have spots like this one. Some have stripes!

The ladybird's hard back is really a pair of wings. They make a strong shield to keep the ladybird safe.

When a ladybird wants to fly, its hard front wings swing out to the side. The hard wings do not flap but they help to lift the ladybird into the air.

Underneath the ladybird's hard, round back there are lots of nerves. They help the ladybird to feel the things around it.

This is the ladybird's brain.

Nerves go right down the ladybird's legs. Others go to the tips of its antennae.

These nerves are like telephone wires. They carry messages around the body.

BUTTERFLY

This butterfly is called a Lime Swallowtail. It flits from flower to flower sipping the nectar. Its wings are brightly coloured, so birds peck at them rather than at its head and body.

When the butterfly feeds, it uncurls this long tube and uses it like a straw to suck up the flower's sweet nectar.

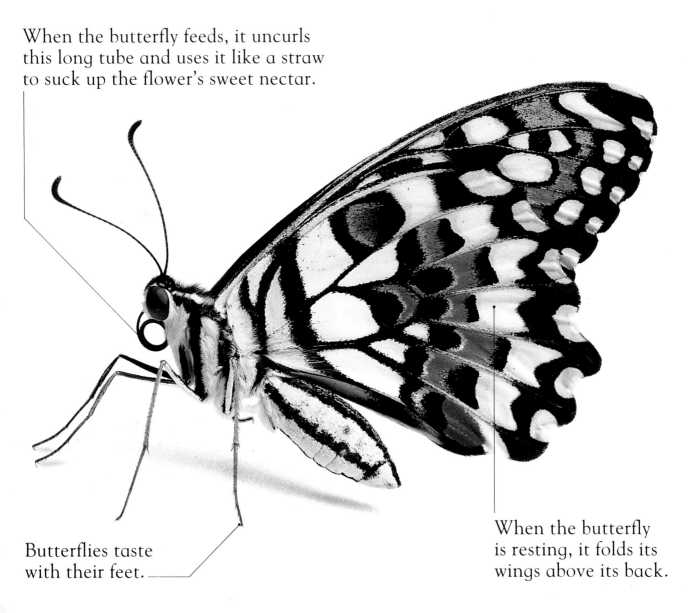

Butterflies taste with their feet.

When the butterfly is resting, it folds its wings above its back.

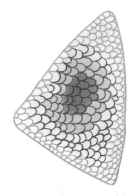

If you look closely through a magnifying glass, you can see that the butterfly's wings are covered with tiny scales. They overlap each other like the tiles on a roof.

The antennae help butterflies to smell flowers.

These supports are like bones – they keep the wings spread out.

Spit is made here and mixed with the food to make it easier to swallow.

This is the butterfly's stomach, where it digests food.

STICK INSECT

If you saw this spiny stick insect on a tree, you might think she was just a dried-up leaf. She can't fly away from danger, so she has to hide herself from birds and lizards. She moves slowly and sways as she walks, so that she looks like part of the tree moving in the wind.

She curls her body so that it looks like the stinging tail of a scorpion.

These sharp spines can give you a nasty prick.

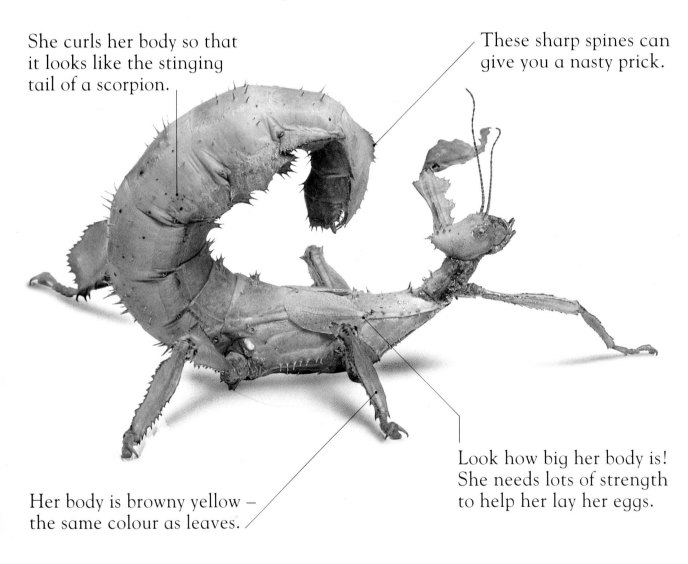

Her body is browny yellow – the same colour as leaves.

Look how big her body is! She needs lots of strength to help her lay her eggs.

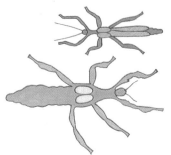

The female spiny stick insect is much bigger than the male.

Ovaries produce the eggs, which pass down the passage to the opening at the end of the tail.

The eggs come out here.

The stick insect uses these muscles to bend her body round.

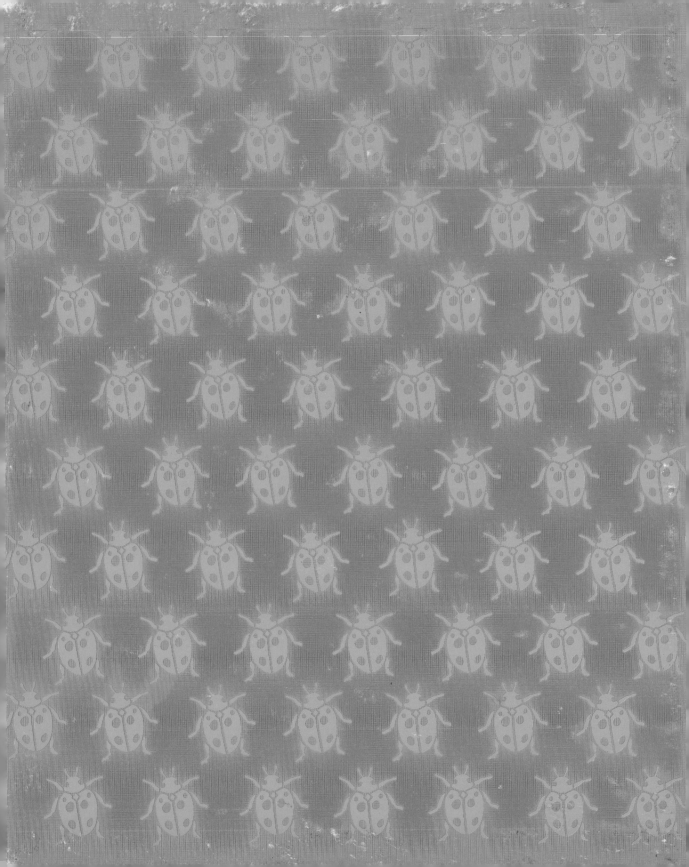